I0099466

MCRP 6-12C

The Commander's Handbook for Religious Ministry Support

U.S. Marine Corps

PCN 144 000090 00

To Our Readers

Changes: Readers of this publication are encouraged to submit suggestions and changes that will improve it. Recommendations may be sent directly to Commanding General, Marine Corps Combat Development Command, Doctrine Division (C 42), 3300 Russell Road, Suite 318A, Quantico, VA 22134-5021 or by fax to 703-784-2917 (DSN 278-2917) or by E-mail to **morgann@mccdc.usmc.mil**. Recommendations should include the following information:

- Location of change
  Publication number and title
  Current page number
  Paragraph number (if applicable)
  Line number
  Figure or table number (if applicable)
- Nature of change
  Add, delete
  Proposed new text, preferably double-
    spaced and typewritten
- Justification and/or source of change

Additional copies: A printed copy of this publication may be obtained from Marine Corps Logistics Base, Albany, GA 31704-5001, by following the instructions in MCBul 5600, *Marine Corps Doctrinal Publications Status.* An electronic copy may be obtained from the Doctrine Division, MCCDC, world wide web home page which is found at the following universal reference locator: **http://www.doctrine.usmc.mil**.

Unless otherwise stated, whenever the masculine gender
is used, both men and women are included.

DEPARTMENT OF THE NAVY
Headquarters United States Marine Corps
Washington, D.C. 20380-1775

2 February 2004

FOREWORD

Successful commanders have discovered that effective use of their Religious Ministry Teams (RMTs) has a positive impact on readiness, moral, and family support issues. They also understand that an effective Command Religious Program (CRP) and the spiritual care that chaplains provide are irreplaceable on the battlefield.

Marine Corps Reference Publication (MCRP) 6-12C, *The Commander's Handbook for Religious Ministry Support*, is a common-sense guide designed for field grade commanders to help facilitate their CRP and to empower their chaplains and RMTs. As a part of the Marine Corps Religious Ministry family of publications, it summarizes information contained in Marine Corps Warfighting Publication (MCWP) 6-12, *Religious Ministry Support in the U.S. Marine Corps*, which is crucial for commanders to become leaders in their CRP.

I commend this publication to all commanders to better use their CRP and to train Navy chaplains for responsible positions in the operating forces.

EDWARD HANLON, JR.
Lieutenant General, U.S. Marine Corps
Commanding General
Marine Corps Combat Development Command

Publication Control Number 144 000090 00

Table of Contents

Chapter 5. Accommodation Issues and Frequently Asked Questions

Appendices

Chapter 1
Spirituality and Warfare

There are only two forces in the world, the sword and the spirit. In the long run the sword will always be conquered by the spirit.

—Napoleon Bonaparte

Lieutenant Colonel Ray Murray commanded the 5th Marines at the Chosin Reservoir. Reflecting on leadership during the fighting withdrawal from this hellish deathtrap he said, "I personally felt in a state of shock, the kind of shock one gets from some great personal tragedy, the sudden loss of someone close. My first fight was within myself. I had to rebuild that emptiness of spirit."[1]

The rebuilding that Lieutenant Colonel Murray refers to is replenishing the spirit. He was referring to his own spiritual life and how important it is to keep that aspect of our life intact in spite of the chaos that surrounds us. We call that spiritual readiness. This chapter will address spiritual readiness and what it has to offer Marines.

Spiritual Readiness

Spirituality begins when a person searches for religious faith. Paradoxically, spirituality is a private matter acted out in a public way. Spiritual readiness renders a Marine capable of coping with any crisis. It is inner self that is tough without being cold. Spiritual readiness is the quality of a Marine's inner self that distinguishes between courage and recklessness. It is an aspect of leadership that is as important as physical readiness or training. Spiritual readiness is the bedrock upon which the concepts of honor, courage, and commitment are built.

In combat, the words "honor, courage, and commitment," are more than a slogan. They are the ideals by which we live and die. To hope when all seems hopeless, to fight on when all seems lost, these are the attributes of the spiritually ready. Only the spiritually ready have the moral courage to persevere in the face of overwhelming odds.

Spirituality is developed in pain and forged in adversity. A person who has lived a sheltered life generally lacks spiritual depth. The term "spirituality" is frequently used but is hard to define. Spirituality is an intangible part of life, very important but difficult to pin down. Some Marines will come to the battlefield with spirituality they developed in a religious upbringing. Some will find their faith reinforced, others will find their faith tested to the breaking point. Some Marines will develop a "battlefield spirituality" that is similar to the coping skills of combat veterans of every war. The adage "religion is for people who don't want to go to hell, spirituality is for people who have already been" finds resonance with some Marines who have experienced a difficult past and are living a painful present.

Drawing on internal resources under hellish circumstances is the connection between spirituality and warfare. The Crucible was developed to push recruits to the lowest depth in order to glimpse the depravations of combat conditions. The Crucible helps recruits realize they will need inner resources to cope with combat. Warfare is extremely stressful for those going through it, and it leaves painful memories in its wake. Combat and its threat of death have a spiritual nature that leaves those who experience it, as Oliver Wendell Homes described, "touched by fire." But warfare can also be spiritually damaging. Eugene Sledge, a World War II Marine mortarman, entitled his book about his experience in the Pacific campaigns, *With The Old Breed At Peleliu and Okinawa.*[2] In it he describes island combat with all the stress and horror that he can convey. Sledge quotes Siegfried Sassoon, a poet and World War I British infantry officer, who returned from the war and penned this verse:

*You smug-faced crowds with kindling eye
Who cheer when soldier lads march by,
Sneak home and pray you'll never know
The hell where youth and laughter go.*

Moral Courage

Sledge also relates an incident from the landing on Peleliu. Peleliu was his first battle, and after several days Sledge was, by his own account, so brutalized by what he had seen that other Marines abusing Japanese corpses no longer bothered him.

I noticed gold teeth glistening brightly between the lips of several of the dead Japanese lying around us. Harvesting gold teeth was one facet of stripping enemy dead that I hadn't practiced so far. But stopping beside a corpse with a particularly tempting number of shining crowns, I took out my kabar and bent over to make the extractions.
A hand grasped me by the shoulder, and I straightened up to see who it was. "What are you gonna do, Sledgehammer?" asked Doc Caswell. His expression was a mix of sadness and reproach as he looked at me.
"Just thought I'd collect some gold teeth," I replied.
"Don't do it."
"Why not, Doc?"
"You don't want to do that sort of thing. What would your folks think if they knew?"
"Well, my dad's a doctor, and I bet he'd think it was kinda interesting," I replied, bending down to resume my task.
"No! The germs, Sledgehammer! You might get germs from them."
I stopped and looked inquiringly at Doc and said, "Germs? Gosh, I never thought of that."
"Yeah, you got to be careful about germs around all these dead Nips, you know," he said vehemently.
"Well, then, I guess I'd better just cut off the insignia on his collar and leave his nasty teeth alone. You think that safe, Doc?"
"I guess so," he replied with an approving nod.
Reflecting on this episode after the war, I realized that Doc Caswell didn't really have germs in mind. He was a good friend and a fine, genuine person whose sensitivity hadn't been crushed out by the war. He was merely trying to help me retain some of mine and not become completely callous and harsh.[3]

This story illustrated spiritual readiness. The company corpsman retained his spiritual readiness and with it his moral courage. He was able to pull the young Marine back from committing an act that would have haunted him for years.

Spiritual readiness is an elusive quality but still real. Spiritual readiness is a force multiplier and is the foundation of moral courage. Moral courage for Marines comes from accepting two truths. The first is that some things are right and we must do these things, no matter what the cost. The second is that some things are wrong and we should never permit them, no matter what the circumstances.

These two truths may seem simplistic and so obvious as to appear foolish. Not so. The boot camp emphasis on core values speaks clearly to a generation that has grown up without moral absolutes. Many of our young Marines grew up without the structure of accountability from home, school or religion. The idea and teaching of Core Values seeks to fill a void that many Marines were not provided with in early development. After they leave the structure of boot camp and their drill instructor, they need to see core values constantly played out in living examples by their chain of command. This is easier said than done. To live out Core Values within a command requires the commander to exercise courage, insight, and compassion. Done well, such a command will be renowned for its climate of integrity, justice, ethics, and esprit de corps.[4]

Among other things, moral courage gives Marines the strength to put the horrors of the battlefield in proper prospective. General Robert E. Lee's statement, "It is well that war is so terrible, or we may grow too fond of it," is an example of a moral man wrestling with a paradox: the joy of victory versus the horror of a battlefield.

Another kind of moral courage is illustrated by this story from World War II. During the Battle of Bastogne, an entire Army

Division lay under siege. Lieutenant Colonel (later General and Army Chief of Staff) Creighton Abrams chose to disobey his orders concerning his supporting role in the rescue when he saw an opportunity to charge straight into Bastogne and break the siege. His Army Commander, General George Patton, noted that not many commanders have that kind of moral courage.[5]

Moral courage gives us the ability to act rightly in a world that is not right. It gives one the ability to act humanely in the midst of inhumanity. While the traits of moral courage and spiritual readiness mean many things to many people, Marines in combat have their own definitions: first, warfare contains unforgettable misery; second, the demands of duty outweigh comfort. Accepting these personal sacrifices as a choice made freely, even while suffering the consequences, is a mark of spiritual readiness. Marines who cannot admit the burden of duty or the spiritual battering they receive in combat are more likely to break down than Marines who have realistic expectations.

While no one can be made completely ready for combat, there are some hallmarks of Marines who are spiritually ready to—

ı Self-motivate.
ı Persist against frustration.
ı Take responsibility.
ı Delay gratification.
ı Remain humble.
ı Stay dedicated to duty.
ı Empathize.
ı Control impulse.
ı Hope.[6]

A Vietnam veteran who experienced trauma was able to find strength because he was spiritually ready:

On the 19th of May, I was shot in the leg and chest. My company was all pinned down by mortar fire. When the men were able to come out to get me, two men lay next to me dead and the other had lost an ear. I had been hit 11 more times.

I think that 99 percent of man's prayer is an unconscious act. As far as my own prayer, up until that day in May, I know in my heart I just went through the steps on the outside. But as I lay there that day and felt the warm blood of life flow from my body, I began to pray to God for the very first time. I spoke to God and felt Him around me. I told him [the chaplain] I knew the Lord was with me, and He would protect me from then on.

—Sgt Stephen M. Malley USMC[7]

The following chapters are a guide to getting your command spiritually ready for warfare.

Chapter 2
Your Command Religious Program

A leader is a dealer in hope.

—Napoleon Bonaparte

The church for the Shanghai-based Fourth Marines operated from whatever movie theater the chaplain could secure. On Christmas Day 1932, the 4th Marines church remembered the children in the Russian Refugee School and in the China Christian Day Nursery. Marines brought over 1,000 presents to the church. Two Christmas trees stood in the lobby of the Cathay Theater, aglow with lights and resplendent with toys, dolls, and varied-colored decorations.[8]

Part of the Command Climate

Marine Corps Order (MCO) 1730.6D, *Command Religious Programs in the Marine Corps*, states "Commanders are responsible for establishing and maintaining a Command Religious Program (CRP) which supports the free exercise of religion as set forth in Secretary of the Navy Instruction (SECNAVINST) 1730.7B, *Religious Ministry Support within the Department of the Navy (DON)*. Commands shall include the CRP as an integral and essential element of their administrative, planning, programming, and budgeting activities."

Often times commanders think of the CRP as only affecting the chaplain and the Marines who go to church. The CRP is more than that; it is a caretaker and truth-teller with regard to a command's spiritual readiness. The chaplain is a subordinate player in the CRP. The principal agent is the commander. All the leaders in the command have a part to play in spiritual readiness. A commander can assess the command's spiritual readiness by answering these questions:

। How many nonjudicial punishments (NJPs) are you holding?

। How often does your unit show up on the blotter?

। How many pre-end of active service (EAS) separations are pending?

। Who is reenlisting? Who is getting out?

। What is attendance like when the key volunteers hold a meeting? Why?

We do not live in a zero-defect world. There are no zero-defect commands. Even the best commands will have Marines who are immature and their trials and tribulations will consume your time and patience. Other Marines are just not prepared for life in the Corps. If some indicators listed above are blatant, the CRP may be able to help.

MCO 1730.6D states that the CRP include "Programs of instruction and other activities that provide family team building enrichment, marriage preparation, moral and ethical development, and suicide awareness from a religious perspective." In most commands, the chaplain is deeply involved in all of these things and more; however, Marine leaders are not always personally involved in these programs. However, when the commander becomes involved, it usually catches the unit's attention. For example: a commander and his wife attended the on-base marriage enrichment training. They spent 2 days in civilian clothes, listened to the material, and then joined in on the discussions along with younger attendees. This commander shared what he got out of the training at the next staff meeting and at the next new-join brief. The next month that unit's attendance at the marriage enrichment seminar tripled. The Marines who would have refused to go because they believed that attendance at such an event signaled that their marriage was in trouble, overcame their reservations and signed up. This created a ripple effect and within 6 months nearly the entire command had attended the marriage enrichment seminar. The command's chaplain noticed a measurable drop in "crisis" marriage counseling.

Thus, leadership has a human face. Sometimes the only human face a junior Marine sees within "the system" is the chaplain. While the chaplain may try to be a friend, he is not the leader. Examples abound of leadership with a human face in every Marine Corps unit, but they are discreet and easy to miss.

Another example of putting a human face on leadership is that of the staff noncommissioned officer (SNCO) who, while giving a junior Marine a "page 11," revealed that early on he had a few "Page 11s" himself, along with an NJP. These events didn't end his life or his career, but in fact served to give him the wake-up-call he needed to get on with life. In a moment, the SNCO went from being just another "lifer" to a true role model. Instead of losing respect for telling about his mistakes, the SNCO gained respect in the young Marines eyes. His seniors weren't perfect; their growing up in the Marines had included some bumps and scrapes. Seeing this, the junior Marine could view the "page 11" as the wake-up-call he needed to move on.

Consider the colonel (a group commander) who concluded an officer professional military education (PME) by telling a story about how he had put in a resignation letter as a captain. Dissatisfied in his unit and the Marine Corps, he decided it was time to move on. With his discharge date approaching, he had a chance conversation with a general officer he respected that caused him to change his mind. When asked why he was leaving, the young captain told the general that he was tired of being in an outfit that cared more about looking good than being good. Instead of being offended, the general responded by asking him to stay on active duty because the Marines needed more officers with that kind of passion, not less. If the captain stayed, he could help turn the problem around. The group commander then went on to explain how he processed the decision to leave and balanced it against the decision to stay and serve. The junior officers in the command were intrigued by this talk in much the same way the junior Marine was in the previous story. Their seniors had also been disappointed with no-liberty deployments and stubborn monitors. But they had made a choice to withstand the disappointment in the short run to enjoy a profession what was satisfying in the long run.

What has this got to do with the CRP? Everyday your chaplain talks to Marines who are fed up with the Corps. They will tell the chaplain things they would never tell their chain of command. While the chaplain cannot break confidence by telling the stories he hears, the chaplain can talk to the commander about some of the themes or situations he is hearing. This provides the commander with information from within his command that he can't get anywhere else.

All of this illustrates the need for the commander to listen to the chaplain. It is also as important for the chaplain to spend time with the commander and the staff. Civilian ministry has no position that prepares a minister to be a military chaplain. For this reason, allowing the chaplain to take part in staff discussions and planning is a valuable part of his orientation to the Marine Corps.

What the Chaplain Can Do

The following describes the most typical functiors of your chaplain; not an inclusive list of everything your chaplain does on a daily, weekly or occasional basis.

Pastoral Counseling

The typical chaplain serving with the Marines spends the majority of his time performing pastoral counseling. The reasons for this are that the majority of the command is comprised of young people who are away from home and now learning from painful experiences. Many of them have never handled their own finances and may be newly married. Their problems are not overtly religious, but they do have a spiritual dimension. They need to talk to an adult they can trust to care for them. This also happens outside the military; many civilian ministers refer to this type of nonreligious pastoral counseling as reparenting. On these issues, most Marines feel more comfortable talking with their chaplain than anyone else. While Marine Corps Community Services (MCCS) also offers counseling, the chaplain works to bring religious faith into every counseling session. The topics in these sessions range from homicide, suicide, and child abuse to Marines who need to blow off some steam. While the command benefits from its chaplain counseling, if the counseling load is overwhelming, the other aspects of the chaplain's ministry will suffer. The chaplain may need to refer Marines and their family members to a health care provider but is reluctant to do this because he feels he is letting the Marines down. In these cases, the chaplain needs to remember to get out and spend time with Marines who are happy with life and their careers. The chaplain needs to remember not to let the urgent outweigh the important and to see and be seen by Marines who don't drop by his office.

Emergency Notifications

Chaplains take part in the casualty assistance calls officer (CACO) process as described in MCO P3040.4D, *Marine Corps Causalty Procedures*. The chaplain accompanies the CACO for initial notification for pastoral care and spiritual support. The chaplain is not the CACO. The family may be able to accept comfort from the person who delivered the bad news, but not always.

Chaplains have also taken part in the delivery of American Red Cross messages. As in the case of a CACO visit, after the officer or SNCO makes the notification, the chaplain is available for pastoral care. Occasionally, the American Red Cross requests that a chaplain deliver the news to the Marine personally. In these cases the chaplain should make the notification along with other members of the chain of command, unless bringing the Marine and the chaplain together is too time consuming and would interfere with the Marine taking leave, etc.

Suicide Prevention and Awareness

Chaplains can provide suicide prevention and awareness workshops. A successful approach is to have medical and the chaplain as a team. Each discipline can approach the subject from different angles, medical and spiritual aspects. The chaplain is often the command's first line of defense in suicide prevention. The Marines are usually comfortable speaking with the chaplain and trust his advice. Depression and thoughts of death have spiritual and theological aspects that a chaplain can help the Marines sort through. What typically happens is that a depressed young person is having adjustment problems and, for the first time in his life, the idea of killing himself crosses his mind. Depressed and scared, he turns to the chaplain. Usually after a few visits, the Marine is adapting to his new setting and is handling stress better. However, if the Marine will not make a pact to live (a promise not to harm himself) or is acting too depressed to be alone, the chaplain will have the Marine taken to medical.

> *NOTE: If the leader sees a Marine acting depressed or out of character, and the Marine either cannot respond or gives inappropriate answers to questions, the leader should take the Marine directly to medical to be seen by a medical officer. The escort Marine should expect to stay with him until relieved. The chaplain does not need to be the middleman in these cases.*

Memorial Services and Funerals

No occasion other than combat requires more from the commander and the chaplain than how they conduct themselves after the death of one of their Marines. The Marines are looking for leadership, reassurance, and closure. This publication cannot contain all the lessons learned from memorial services and funerals; the following are the most important.

The commander and the chaplain should meet and have the service scripted out at least 2 days ahead of time. If your command has standing operating procedures for these services, get a copy and review it. If the chaplain needs a few hands to help square away the chapel before and after, make sure he gets some of your best. If the chaplain has never done this type of service with the Marines, get him to call his supervisor chaplain for some pointers.

The Marines will be paying very close attention to the service. Most of the seats in the chapel will be filled with first-term Marines who have come to pay respects to another first-term Marine. The care, concern, and pride displayed by the commander and the chaplain to the deceased and his family will remind the Marines that they are in a brotherhood.

Religious Services

As a result of Chaplain Corps policy, chaplains assigned to the base handle all on-base services. The majority of chaplains serving in the operating forces only hold services when they are in the field. Services in the field should be held on Sunday if operationally feasible. If not, then time should be allowed for the religious ministry team (RMT) to set up church and the word to get out so Marines can attend. In a spiritual sense, services in the field gives the chaplain a chance to practice preventative maintenance vice repair. Done well, a field service is a joyful experience. For some attendees, it could be their first church service.

Humanitarian Transfers and Hardship Discharges

Chaplains are not the official starting point in this process, but can assist in requesting humanitarian transfers and hardship discharges. This assistance is not intended to relieve the chain of command of its responsibilities. Too many times when a Marine asks his leader about one of these administrative actions, the leader replies, "Go see the chaplain." Every Marine should be interviewed by his noncommissioned officer (NCO), SNCO, and platoon commander. There are two reasons for this: first, the Marine needs to know that his chain of command is interested in his problems; second, in leadership development, the sooner that the NCOs and lieutenants grasp an understanding of the documentation process, MCOs, etc., the better. They will be deeply involved in these administrative actions when they become senior Marines and they need to learn procedures. Chaplains can help both the Marine and the chain of command as a resource.

These two administrative actions—humanitarian transfer and hardship discharges—can be the most rewarding and most frustrating things the chaplain deals with. It can be rewarding when there is a true need and the chaplain helps facilitate the action. It can also be rewarding when the chaplain helps the individual with the problem find a solution that negates a transfer or discharge. The frustrating part is when an individual fabricates a problem or aggravates a situation to get a transfer or discharge. In either case, in order to be effective, the chaplain should first get the individual to sign a release of confidentially. This is so the chaplain can speak freely, yet discretely, to the chain of command about the Marine and his issues.

Family Readiness

Premarital Preparation

Chaplains conduct premarital counseling and preparation based on their experience and faith group requirements. Every Marine base chapel program has some type of premarital class. Many commanders offer enticements, such as Fridays off for the young Marines to attend premarital classes. The program that Navy chaplains employ as both marital and premarital counseling is the Prevention and Relationship Enhancement Program (PREP). PREP is based on 20 years of research by the University of Colorado on what makes marriages last. PREP is designed for married couples who want to communicate better but it is also outstanding for engaged couples who are serious about premarital preparation. MCCS offers other types of premarital counseling such as budgeting, etc.

Marriage Counseling

In some commands, marriage counseling can easily become the chaplain's most time-consuming task. Since chaplains are compassionate people by nature and want to help, it can become easy for them to become almost full time marriage counselors. As a commander you cannot allow this to happen. If the chaplain is spending more than 50 percent of his/her day counseling for a prolonged period, something is wrong. If a couple still needs counseling after two or three visits, unless the couple and the chaplain believe they are making real progress, the couple should be referred to a professional counselor.

While MCCS performs marriage counseling, many couples have found a 48-hour marriage enrichment weekend with the Chaplains Religious Enrichment Development Operation (CREDO) enhanced their marriages. CREDO is availabnle at or near all major bases.

Family Violence Intervention/Family Advocacy

Chaplains are often the first resource in family violence. Their actions can range from encouraging offenders to seek assistance through self-referral to assisting a non-military spouse and children into a shelter or returning to their home of record.

The professional and legal requirements of maintaining the seal of privileged communication in such circumstances are the basis for the Marine Corps policy that prevents chaplairs from serving as a command's family advocacy point of contact, program manager or program official.

The commander needs to recognize that when chaplains are used as a resource in family violence, this often creates a dilemma for the chaplain. When the episode is reported to the chaplain in a setting of privileged communication, the chaplain can urge the person, be they victim or victimizer, to go forward and get appropriate help. But the chaplain can only urge or encourage the appropriate action; the chaplain cannot be the person who reports to the authorities.

What the Chaplain Cannot Do

The following feats are examples of what chaplains are sometimes asked to help with. While a chaplain might be able to assist or offer sage advice, the following are not within the scope of ministry:

ı   Chaplains cannot obtain special consideration for moving into military housing.

ı   Chaplains cannot obtain special medical care or privileges.

ı   Chaplains cannot provide immediate financial aid or food. Chaplains can steer those in need toward Navy and Marine Corps Relief or another charity.

ı   Chaplains should not be asked to use influence to change orders or sway monitors.

ı   Chaplains are prohibited from leading a fund drive or handling money.

What the Command Religious Program Needs from the Commander

Supplies

Marine Corps Reference Publications (MCRP) 6-12A, *Religious Ministry Team Handbook,* goes into detail about RMT supplies. The RMT mount-out box is an inspection item for the commanding general's readiness inspection (CGRI). However the mount-out box is not included in the table of equipment, nor does it have a table of authorized material control number assigned. Your chaplain, with the advice of the major subordinate command (MSC) chaplain, will have no problem keeping it stocked in garrison. In a combat zone, however, the religious supplies go fast. The RMT may need some assistance from the S-4 in getting resupply from the "God Block" on Military Sealift Command ships or from continental United States to the front.

Training

Your chaplain needs to keep his ministry skills current. The Navy Chaplain Corps offers annual training called Professional Development Training Course (PDTC) that is held aboard the major Marine and Navy bases. The topics change every year and your chaplain is required to go unless he is deployed. The Navy Chaplain Corps also hosts workshops usually lasting a day or two that are conducted at major bases. These have relevant topics that will help your chaplain perform ministry in his unit. The chaplain also has to stay in touch with his endorsing agent. This is the representative from religious body that has accredited him to the military ministry. He may be required to go on retreats or conferences.

When your chaplain goes to one of these, they will come back refreshed and reenergized. When the chaplain gets fresh ideas for ministry in the command, he is a force enabler.

Orientation

The majority of chaplains will never receive advanced military education such as joint professional military education, Command and Staff College, etc. Their real military education will come from you and the staff. During the chaplain's first tour with Marines, he should become acquainted with concepts such as: timed-phased force and deployment data (TPFDD), the different levels of war, and the planning that goes into them. Many junior chaplains never receive this type of orientation and wish they had when they become senior chaplains serving with Marines. A measurable goal for the commander and the chaplain to reach in orientation would be for the chaplain to understand what is being discussed in staff meetings. The commander and staff can assist the new chaplain understand military issues such as organizational structures, chain of command, how units interact and support each other, safety, what to bring to the field, etc. The time spent in helping the chaplain understand staffing and planning issues will enhance his contribution to the command and help other commanders down the road.

Chapter 3
The Religious Ministry Team

*Even though I walk through the valley of the shadow of death, I
will fear no evil, for you are with me; your rod and your staff they
comfort me.*

—Psalm 23

Enlisted Marines assigned to chaplains at Khe Sanh suffered great
losses. In addition to Private First Class (PFC) Alexander Chin
who was killed along with Chaplain Brett, Chaplain Hampton lost
his clerk, and Chaplain Stubbe, who was without a clerk at the
beginning of the battle, had PFC Spicer transferred to him.
Spicer, a mild-mannered and caring person, frequently threw himself over the bodies of causalities during incoming, and during
one evacuation of wounded, was fatally wounded.[9]

Chaplain Skills: Functions and Tasks

The Chaplain Corps has instituted a program called Standards for
Ministry. This does not mean that every chaplain's ministry will
look the same. It simply means that just as every Basic School graduate has a skill set they can draw from, Navy chaplains—whether
Protestant, Catholic, Jewish or Muslim—all have a skill set that
they can perform from. The Standards for Ministry have been broken down into functions and tasks. MCRP 6-12A details each function and describes the embedded tasks. Following are the six
functions with a brief summation of the tasks.

Command Advisory

Advise the command on moral, ethical, cultural, and religious issues. (See chapter 4.)

Religious Ministry and Accommodation

Assess, identify, and research command religious faith group requirements. Develop programs to facilitate individual and group religious expression and accommodation. (See chapter 5.)

Outreach

Develop, plan, and coordinate for religious ministries programs and spiritual growth programs.

Pastoral Care

Provide pastoral counseling, crisis prevention, spiritual direction, mentoring, and pastoral support for ceremonies.

Training and Education

Provide command-wide education and training from a religious perspective on ethics, cross-cultural issues, relational and life skills, personal and spiritual readiness, suicide prevention, domestic violence, moral issues, and religious education.

Supervisory and Management

Plan and provide for the professional development of all assigned personnel.

Marine Skills: An Expeditionary Ministry

By Marine Corps policy and doctrine, the chaplain and the Religious Program Specialist (RP) work together as an RMT. Unless RMT members had prior Marine tours, they will need orientation from the commander and staff. Entry-level training for chaplains and RPs takes place at the Chaplain and RP Expeditionary Skills Training (CREST) course at Camp Lejeune, NC. Once assigned to a unit in the Marine operating forces, the RMT needs to keep building on the foundation of these core field skills for the remainder of their tour. The RMT should accompany the command to the field. If an element of the command, such as a company, is spending a week in the field, the battalion RMT should spend a day and night with them. The RMT needs to stay current with how the Marines are trained and to interact with them.

As a noncombatant, the chaplain is prohibited from carrying a weapon. (SECNAVINST 1730.7) The RP is a combatant and should be as qualified with his/her issued weapon as any Marine. (MCO 3574.2J, *Entry Level and Sustainment Level MarksmanshipTraining with the M16A2 Service Rifle and M9 Service Pistol)* In several instances, RPs have locked and loaded and taken defensive positions alongside the Marines.

For chaplains, taking water survival classes and going to the nuclear, biological, and chemical (NBC) chamber do more than teach survival skills. Many positive ministry opportunities occur after Marines witness their chaplain struggling alongside them.

In the past, RPs serving with Marines focused on force protection for the chaplain alone. This is no longer true. The RP should be used in positions consistent with rank and experience. While it may take longer to train an RP3 to patrol the defensive perimeter than an experienced corporal, RPs are combatants and can be expected to impact in the unit's mission beyond what they do in the RMT.

Mindset

As per basis skills training, the commander should expect that the RMT will perform Marine Corps Common Skills better than a new recruit; however, the RMT members are not infantrymen. The RMT needs help and advice from the commander in developing an expeditionary mindset. The RMT must always be deployment ready materially, administratively, and mentally. The supervisor chaplain (division, wing, force service support group) and the inspection system in place is adequate to ensure that the RMT's materials are deployment ready. But only the commander and his staff, executive officer, S-3, sergeant major, etc., can give the RMT the situational awareness needed to function in a real world contingency. If the command is deployed and then folded into a Marine expeditionary brigade, division, joint task force, etc., the RMT will have ministry functions beyond the team's parent command.

When deployed to an area of operations (AO) the RMT will likely be tasked to provide ministry in a joint, interagency, and perhaps multinational environment. The RMT needs to know how to effectively balance requests for services and communicate with their parent command if they move around the AO. The chaplain should brief the commander daily on what the RMT is doing inside and outside the command's lifelines.

The mindset for ministry in an expeditionary environment is one that is:

ı Interoperable.

ı Flexible.

ı Capable of operating effectively in uncertainty.

ı With complementary capabilities.

ı An art, not a science.

RMT in Combat

The following section pertains to the entire Marine expeditionary force (MEF). However, it is of particulate relevance to the ground combat element. While it is impossible to cover every circumstance in combat, the following serves as basis for deploying the RMT in combat.

In either the offensive or defensive, chaplains provide their commanders with verbal updates whenever possible, keeping them informed of the RMT's location, communication, transportation plans, and concerns.

Offensive

When possible, the RMT should stay between the company officer's command post and the casualty collection point so the RMT can keep up with the tempo of the assault and, if there are casualties, minister to the wounded. The chaplain should maintain a ministry of presence, seeing as many as possible, but realizing that the RMT cannot be everywhere at once. Ministry in this setting is not the time to hold a formal divine service; the chaplain will mostly be offering words of encouragement and prayers. If there are reconnaissance or security forces going out, the chaplain will be available to be with them before they step off. The RMT should not hover around the commander, but be easily located and accessible.

Defensive

If the unit is dug in and not taking casualties, the RMT should move from unit to unit providing ministry of presence, taking meals, spending the night, etc. If the command is taking casualties, the RMT should stay at the casualty collection point or battalion aid station and provide ministry to the wounded.

Actions Below the Battalion Level

When combat actions are below the battalion level, how to best deploy and employ the chaplain is an issue. For the chaplain to experience a patrol would give him valuable insight to what the Marines experience. However, when the chaplain is out operating with a company or a platoon, he is not available for the rest of the battalion.

When Lieutenant Colonel Hal Moore led the 1st Battalion, 7th Cavalry (1/7) into Vietnam's Ia Drang Valley in November 1965, he made a deliberate decision to leave the battalion chaplain back at the base camp. His reasoning was that since he only had one chaplain, the medical evacuation patients needed him more than the troops in battle. This may have been true, but was the effect of that decision that the chaplain became an "outsider" because he wasn't there? While few battalions will be in an action as violent and prolonged as 1/7, the commander and the chaplain should have an understanding that includes the chaplain going out on some patrols, but knowing there will be times the chaplain may be left in the rear.

Military Operations Other Than War

Military operations other than war (MOOTW) presents opportunities for the chaplain to support the mission in ways that are vastly different than being in combat. This issue is addressed in chapter 4 and also in MCWP 3-33.1, *MAGTF Civil-Military Operations*. During MOOTW there might be situations where your Marines are in condition 2 and the chaplain is defusing a situation with some of the nationals.

Preventing Combat Stress

Combat stress is the mental, emotional or physical tension, strain or distress resulting from exposure to combat and combat-related conditions. An example of combat-related conditions would include a MOOTW that involved Marines seeing civilian casualties, a stressful noncombatant evacuation order, etc. Not all combat stress involves actual combat. Historically, rates of combat stress casualties vary greatly, with higher ratios during lengthy periods of intense combat. On Okinawa in 1945, during one peak month of battle, the combat stress casualties among Marines were reported as high as one for every two wounded in action. (MCRP 6-11C, *Combat Stress*)

After an engagement, there will be Marines looking for answers. Many Marines who have never given faith, religion or the meaning of life a second thought will want to talk to the chaplain. Grief, anger, and fear are among the emotions combat veterans experience. In order to be effective across the entire command, the RMT will practice a type of triage, just as medical does. This is where a seasoned RMT that both knows the Marines and is known by them is very valuable. Some Marines need to see the chaplain right away; others can afford to wait. Only an RMT that is active in the life of the command knows the difference.

The chaplain will provide pastoral care to the Marines. As with any traumatic situation, needs will be different. Some Marines will need rest, a hot meal, and a prayer or words of encouragement. Other Marines will need a critical event debriefing as outlined in MCRP 6-11C. The key for the entire chain of command is to know their Marines and to be alert for any sudden, persistent or progressive change in their behavior. The small-unit leader can usually determine if the individual is not performing his duties normally, not taking care of himself, behaving in an unusual fashion, etc.

A leader is not required to have the skills of a psychologist or chaplain. The same ability to observe behavior that applies in suicide intervention applies to combat stress. The leader needs to encourage his Marines to talk about how they perceived an event, e.g., a firefight. Merely talking about what happened can relieve combat stress. In most cases, the young Marines will talk among themselves without any urging. The leader needs to be extraordinarily aware how any of the new replacements, or anyone else who is not apart of the group, or who has not found a buddy yet, is doing. The chaplain will be able to meet with any Marine or group of Marines to talk about what they are experiencing. It may be appropriate for the chaplain to lead a discussion, a religious/memorial service, provide sacraments, etc. When it comes to healing the soul, the Marines and chaplain should remember that working or praying with someone after a horrific situation does not mean that the Marine is now cured. The best outcome is that the events of combat can be put into their proper perspective. Religion contains the power to heal the soul and help Marines cope with what they are experiencing.

Combat stress is not abnormal. Typically, rest, hot food, a chance to unwind, and the leader showing concern, will defuse most combat stress. Sometimes the combat stress is so severe that the Marine needs to be relieved from duty for a few days. In these cases he should go no farther back than necessary. Depending how the medical assets are deployed, the Marine might be seen at the combat support staging area, the nearest Surgical Company, or if necessary, back aboard ship. He may be given medication to help him sleep and have the chance to talk to a member of the mental health team. During this time he will not be treated like a patient or a sick person, but reminded that he is still a Marine and a warfighter. If treated near their units, 65 to 85 percent of combat stress casualties return to duty in 1 to 3 days. The more quickly those with mild combat stress are returned to full duty, the less likely they will have psychiatric problems later. About 15 to 20 percent more return to duty in 1 to 2 weeks. Only 5 to 10 percent are sent home, and these usually have other problems in addition to combat stress reactions. If evacuated, few combat stressed military members will return to duty. In fact, many are likely to be permanently disabled.

Predeployment and Deployment Return and Reunion

Before deployment, the chaplain is just one member of the staff that is helping the command get ready to deploy. Typically the chaplain, the family readiness officer (FRO), and the sergeant major may cover some of the same ground and have multiple visits with the same people. While most experienced chaplains could give an entire predeployment brief themselves, they shouldn't. The FRO, Navy and Marine Corps Relief Society representative, president of the key volunteers, etc., should all play a part. The chaplain normally presents something about the importance of communication, family dynamics, emotional cycle of deployment and how to contact the base chaplains.

Return and reunion briefs are usually more meaningful. At a pre-deployment brief, many of the young Marines and their spouses who are the most likely to have problems are the least likely to pay attention or believe the topic applies to them. At the end of a deployment, many young Marines are sadder but wiser and know the material applies to them. If the deployment has included com-bat, there may be some Marines who will display symptoms of combat stress in the post-deployment stage. CREDO has devel-oped a Mobile CREDO that is able to deploy to where you are. The programs they offer include Warrior Transformation and Operational Stress Control. The CREDO near your base offers programs for spouses affected by deployment stress and Marines returning from a hostile environment. Your chaplain can give you an in-depth brief on the various programs CREDO offers.

Managing the Chaplain and RP

Unless the chaplain and RP have served with Marines before, they will need some help learning the language and tempo of the command. The Chaplain's School and a turnover can only do so much to describe something that has to be experienced to be understood. The best thing that can happen to a new chaplain is to be oriented by the S-3, S-4, and sergeant major. Understanding the operations, training, supply, and personnel aspects of the com-mand will assist the chaplain put it all in perspective. Every effort the staff puts into helping raise the chaplain's staff skills will pay dividends later. Unlike any other new lieutenant, the chaplains do not have a dedicated SNCO to train them.

The RP's situation is similar. Most want to be there and to make a difference, but sometimes may need a little help fitting in. Checking in with one of the SNCOs in administration and training, and attending all meetings that Marines of his pay grade are involved in, are some ways that can bring and keep the RP current. An RP that is tuned into the enlisted network is helpful to the chaplain and can solve problems before they become crises.

The majority of Navy chaplains and RPs serving with the Marine Corps are there because they ask for that assignment. Most will likely say their time with Marines was one of the highpoints of their service. For that reason you want them to get promoted. They need fitness reports that are fair and career enhancing. This topic is one of the biggest intraservice disconnects that Navy chaplains face. The Navy fitness report system is suffering from years of grade inflation. For this reason a report that a Marine commander believes is fair and positive ends up being unhelpful. If the commander wants a chaplain promoted, he should meet with the supervisor chaplain (MEF, division, wing, group) and talk about the report. The supervisor chaplain is likely more in tune with the kind of report selection boards are looking for and can help the commander write a good one.

Unfortunately, there are some chaplains and RPs serving with Marines who are not up to the task. If it seems to be a case of a chaplain who is a little slow coming online, a communication problem, or a personality clash, a counseling session with the commander, the chaplain and the supervisor chaplain may solve the problem. If it is the RP who is having problems, a meeting with the sergeant major and the senior RP may produce results. However, if the problem is not one of orientation but rather one of attitude, the greatest service the commanders can perform for the Marine Corps and the Department of the Navy is send them home—not back to the Navy. If the chaplain or RP can't cut it with the Marines, the Navy doesn't need them. There are other chaplains and Sailors who are willing to serve.

If the commander, along with the senior Navy Chaplain who works directly for the commanding general, believe that a chaplain is not fit for further service, there are two administrative means of putting them out of the Navy.

First, both Department of Defense Instruction (DODI) 1332.40, *Separation Procedures for Regular and Reserve Commission Officers*, and SECNAVINST 1920.6B, *Administrative Separation of Officers,* outline a show-cause board. Second, Navy Military Personnel Command Manual (NAVPER) 15560D, *Navy Military Personnel Manual (MILPERSMAN)* 1611-020, *Officer Detachment for Cause (DFC)*, outlines how an officer is DFC. Understanding these administrative policies will guide the commander in detaching an ineffective chaplain.

Chapter 4
The Chaplain as Command Advisor

Never confuse the spirit of an army with its mood.[10]

—Carl von Clausewitz

The difficulty in distinguishing morale and mood presents significant challenges for the chaplain serving in his role as command advisor. The chaplain should be able to give the commander intelligent feedback about how the Marines are doing. For our purposes we will equate morale with esprit de corps. It is possible for commands to have fine morale and be in a bad mood. It is also possible for commands to be in a good mood and have low morale. The following passage from Eugene Sledge's *With the Old Breed* illustrates how difficult it is to delineate mood from morale. The book recalls a situation during the battle on Okinawa when Sledge's K Company was on the march, battle-weary, hungry, and wet.

As our column moved along the base of a road embankment on one occasion, a Marine walking along the road above us carrying a field telephone and a small roll of wire shouted down and asked for the identity of our unit. His buddy followed him along the road at a little distance carrying a roll of wire. These men were clean-shaven and neat. They looked suspiciously like rear-echelon people to us.

"Hey, what outfit you guys in?" shouted the first man up on the road.

"K/3/5," I yelled.

His buddy behind him asked him, "What outfit did he say?"

"K/3/5, whatever the hell that means."

The effect on us was instant and dramatic. Men who had paid little attention to what seemed a routine inquiry looked angrily up at the man. I flushed with anger. My unit and I had been insulted. The mortarman next to me threw down his ammo bag and started up the embankment.

"I'll show you what the hell it means, you rear-echelon sonofabitch! I'm gonna whip your ass."

I wasn't given to brawling. The Japanese provided me with all the excitement and fighting I wanted. But I lost my head completely. I threw down my ammo bag and started up the embankment. Other mortarmen started up, too.

"What's the dope?" I heard a man back along the column shout.

"That rear-echelon bastard up there cussed K Company," someone answered.

Immediately other Company K men started up the bank. The two men up on the road looked utterly bewildered as they saw bearded, muddy Marine infantrymen cursing, grounding their weapons, dropping their loads, and surging angrily up the embankment... The two men on the road had become frightened, and we saw them hustling along the road to the rear. They looked back anxiously several times to see whether they were being followed. We must have been an angry, menacing-looking bunch from their viewpoint. I suspect those two Marines knew the real meaning and essence of esprit de corps after that experience.[11]

This passage highlights a spirit and pride that is hard to measure in peacetime metrics. It also highlights how hard it is to really read what is going on in a unit unless you are a member of that unit. Your chaplain should work to understand and read the mood and morale of unit. But until he has lived and suffered with them, he won't really know them well enough to be a true judge of how they are doing. The commander who is new, or taking command of a new detachment of Marines is in the same situation. A battalion commander may not know the morale or mood of one of his companies. But he can read the clues and, along with the chaplain and a few other trusted agents, know enough about one of his units to know if there is need for concern.

The principal service that a chaplain provides to a **command** is as a religious leader; the principal service the chaplain provides to an operational **commander** is as an advisor. Historically this role has ranged from being one of the most valuable to being one of the most misunderstood.

There are a multitude of reasons for this, but the major reason has to do with the tension between the chaplain's ministerial calling and his military calling. These two callings are not always a comfortable fit, and they shouldn't be.

Paradoxically, it is this tension that gives the chaplain value as an advisor. The chaplain may see things differently, and the commander should encourage different perspectives. There will be times the chaplain will be one of the consenting voices, and times when he is one of the dissenting voices. Commanders should know that consent does not equal loyalty and dissent does not equal disloyalty. Winston Churchill once wrote to a colleague he disagreed with on an issue; "Let us have differences, not misunderstandings."

The chaplain can be the most effective when he is an active team member of the staff. By maintaining professional relationships and liaison with other staff sections, and by participating in the planning of all training, exercises, deployments, and special events, the chaplain's situational awareness is an enhancement to his dual role as advisor and ministry leader.

Developing the Chaplain as a Command Advisor

There is no civilian ministry job that compares with military ministry. Although the Navy Chaplains School successfully transforms a civilian minister into a military chaplain, the chaplain will still need assistance and development. During the initial interview, the chaplain should be encouraged to become intimately involved in the command. One of the chaplain's greatest assets, the absence of command responsibilities, can allow him to relate to the Marines on their terms, and at their level of perspective. The chaplain will hear or see things that other officers or the sergeant major may not hear or see because of their more formal relationship with the troops. Thus, the chaplain may be capable of providing valuable insight to the commander on the morale and welfare of his Marines. To gain and maintain credibility as a viable part of the command, the chaplain must be seen by the troops in his office, in the field, and during athletic and command events. Chaplains must be visible and approachable. New-join briefs and key volunteer meetings are outstanding venues for the chaplain to meet Marines and their families. As much as possible, the chaplain should become familiar with the families of the Marines to assist with their problems, spiritual and personal needs. He should also regularly visit Marines and their family members who have been hospitalized or are sick in quarters.

Staff Skills

The chaplain is expected to perform as a staff officer. The fastest and most common-sense approach is to ensure he is included in staff meetings and planning sessions. If the staff and subordinate commanders are planning a field exercise, the chaplain should be included. When the chaplain gives a brief or produces a written document, expect it to be of the same quality you would expect for any officer in the same grade. Most chaplains will not attend formal graduate level military education. Their staff knowledge will come from your command and personal attention of your staff and subordinate commanders.

Operational Skills

Command advisement at the operational level includes informing a deployed command of religious and high holy days that will affect Marines and foreign nationals in the AO. For example, advising the command on special considerations that will apply if the deployment takes place in a Muslim country during Ramadan.

The RMT will keep track of religious supplies and, when possible, arrange visits to local houses of worship to accommodate various faith groups.

Ministry Skills

Chaplains can be effective counselors. Some chaplains have specialized training in drug and alcohol abuse, marriage counseling, corrections, group problem solving, etc., but it is unrealistic to expect all chaplains to have expertise in all of these special areas. However, commanders expect chaplains to be qualified pastoral counselors.

Commanders may ask the chaplain to describe the command's morale. Assessing command morale is one of the most difficult aspects of leadership. In normal garrison activities, boredom can impact morale. In combat, understanding morale is paramount.

Chaplains are the commander's principal advisors regarding the spiritual, moral, and ethical implication of command decisions. In some cases they may offer solutions that had not been considered, such as in the following examples.

Example 1

The commander was faced with an ethical dilemma. One of his SNCOs had beaten up his live-in girlfriend. This SNCO was a 27-year Marine who was planning to retire in the next year. To make matters worse, the girlfriend was a high level base employee. To further complicate the issue, the beating occurred on a weekend and, due to some back channel communications, the commanding general knew of the incident before the commander. Before the commander even knew all the facts, he had been told, "not to press the case, and let the command sergeant major handle it." Troubled, he shared his dilemma with the chaplain. They both agreed that while bringing the SNCO up on charges was a distasteful duty, letting him get away with what happened would give a green light to domestic violence and make a mockery of good order and discipline.

Example 2

A popular Marine was killed in an auto accident shortly before his discharge. He was a geographical bachelor, having moved his family back to his home of record a year before. During that year he had gained a girlfriend, also a Marine. To make things worse, he had told her he intended to divorce his wife and marry her. He informed his closest friends that this was a lie told to keep the girlfriend happy. The Marine was to be buried in his hometown on the other side of the country. The girlfriend dropped a set of leave papers and told her chain of command she intended to be at the funeral and tell the wife the truth. She further stated that if her leave papers were denied she would take unauthorized absence (UA) and contact the media.

The commander first denied her leave and looked into ways to put her in pretrial confinement. However base legal nixed this idea; she actually hadn't done anything and now denied ever saying anything about going UA. The entire chain of command agreed that this was the worse dilemma they had ever seen. The commander asked the chaplain to help mediate.

After several painful hours of counseling and negotiating between the commander, the sergeant major, and the Marine, a compromise was struck. She would be allowed to attend the funeral, but under no circumstances was she to speak to the wife or parents.

Cultural and Religious Issues External to the Command

When commands are deployed on foreign soil, religious practices of host nationals, indigenous persons, allied forces, and enemy forces may impact on planning and execution of operations. While few chaplains are world religion experts, most will have a religious/cultural insight that can aid the commander. MCRP 6-12A, appendix B, is the Religious Area Survey. It can be used to raise the chaplain's own situational awareness concerning the local religions and culture and advise the staff accordingly. However, chaplains must be careful when providing information so as not to assume a position of intelligence gathering and violate their status as a noncombatant.

Chaplains in MOOTW: Nongovernmental Organizations/ International Organizations

In recent years commanders have found chaplains to be excellent liaisons with nongovernmental organizations (NGOs) and international organizations (IOs.) If the headquarters has a civil affairs officer, he and the chaplain can be a great asset to the operation by working together. However, if the operation involves a battalion landing team going ashore, for example, and the situation requires interface with NGOs and IOs, the chaplain may be the best officer to work with them. If the chaplain does meet with NGOs and IOs, the commander needs to set the boundaries; for example, the battalion can send up a working party to help repair a school, but cannot provide any building supplies.

Chaplains have also provided valuable service in MOOTW by acting as liaison with local religious leaders. In some parts of the world, religious leaders are the true community leaders and their cooperation is valuable to mission success.

Chapter 5
Accommodation Issues and Frequently Asked Questions

Treat people as if they were what they ought to be and you help them to become what they are capable of being.

—Goethe

MCO 1730.6D, paragraph c, states: "Whenever possible, accommodating individual religious beliefs and practices is encouraged. However, the impact of accommodation must not adversely affect military readiness, individual or unit readiness, unit cohesion, health, safety, or good order and discipline." As MCRP 6-12A, chapter 3, goes into greater detail about all aspects of accommodation, this chapter will not repeat that information. For most bases, stations, and commands within the Marine Corps, accommodating traditional religions in the United States, i.e., Christianity both Catholic and Protestant, and Judaism, has not been an issue. This chapter addresses nontraditional religions and when accommodation is difficult to achieve. This chapter also contains a section of frequently asked questions by commanders.

The diverse demographics of the United States makes for an equally diverse religious makeup in the Marine Corps. The chaplain should be aware of Marines who require special religious accommodation. When the chaplain addresses Marines at the command's new join brief he should ask those with special needs to visit or call him. Chaplains try to maintain the dignity and privacy of everyone, but religious accommodation needs should be disclosed before going to the field or deploying. A brief overview of accommodations follows.

NOTE: To assist commands with accommodation questions, the Navy Chief of Chaplains office maintains The Chaplains Resource Board (CRB) in Norfolk, VA, at website www.chaplain.navy.mil

Accommodations

Dietary Issues

The majority of dietary issues will come from Marines who cannot eat pork for religious reasons. MCO 10110.34E, *US Marine Corps Food and Subsistence Program,* states that, "The menus used in garrison mess halls are of sufficient variety to accommodate most Marines and religious dietary concerns." However, SECNAVINST 1730.8A, *Accommodation of Religious Practices,* authorizes separate rations within the guidelines of DOD 7000.14-R, *Financial Management Regulations* (known as the DOD Pay Manual). Policy and procedure for processing a request for separate rations may include a recommendation from a chaplain who has counseled the applicant. It is advisable that the chaplain contact an authority within the faith group to determine the legitimacy of the request and if alternatives are available according to the dictates of the faith practice. Common sense dictates that separate rations are unnecessary for Marines living off base and unrealistic for Marines living in the barracks. Ideally, the chain of command should ensure the Marine's dietary needs are being met by the dining facility.

Immunizations/DNA Samples

Some Marines have religious reasons for not taking immunizations and giving deoxyribonucleic acid (DNA) samples. The policy governing immunizations is found in Bureau of Medicine and Surgery Instruction (BUMEDINST) 6230.15, *Immunization and Chemoprophylaxix*. Policy and procedure for processing a request for exemption from giving a DNA sample is found in SEC-NAVINST 1730.8A. Normally, an immunization waiver will only be granted if the Marine requesting it will not be a health hazard to others.

Frequently Asked Questions

Chaplains from the three MEFs were asked to consolidate the most frequently asked questions from their commanders.

Q: What makes a military chaplain different from any other minister?

A: Civilian ministers mainly take care of their own. They pastor and teach people who are usually in tune with their theology and world-view. Chaplains serve as staff officers to the command. However they typically only "pastor" to a small group within the command, to use the understanding of the pastoral relationship as it is experienced in civilian ministry. Usually these two roles don't come into conflict, but they can.

EXAMPLE: One Christmas, the battalion choir, an informal group of Marines who liked to sing, approached the chain of command about singing at the pre-Christmas safety stand-down. They were given permission and rehearsed their routine. Some of their songs were written for Christians and the chaplain knew there were Marines present from other religions. The current interpretation of the law is that religious events are designed to for voluntary attendance. The command's safety stand-down was not voluntary, which placed the Christian chaplain in a dilemma. While he personally liked and believed in the message of the Christmas music, he was compelled to advise the commander on the law concerning such events. The commander's decision was to let the choir sing, but limit their program to music with no religious themes. While the choir was upset with the chaplain, the Christians in the choir were outraged. No matter how he tried to explain his responsibility, they felt betrayed.

Q: Why do chaplains have "privileged communication"? How does it differ from the medical term "confidentiality"?

A: Practically speaking, the terms are used interchangeability by chaplains and Marines. However, "confidentiality" is the theological/pastoral term that is technically correct and backed up by the Uniform Code of Military Justice (UCMJ). Military courts have consistently enforced the chaplain-penitent privilege for military chaplains and servicemembers. For chaplains, this means that they cannot give out information without the person's approval. The individual seeking help knows the chaplain can guide him, but the individual "owns" the information of the counseling relationship. MCRP 6-12A, chapter 9, expands on this issue.

Q: How can you (the chaplain) not tell me (the commander) everything about your conversation with an individual Marine? After all, am I not the commanding officer? I should have knowledge of your every conversation if I inquire as it affects my ability to lead this command.

A: The legality of this question was discussed earlier. The commander should look at the long-term vice the short term payoff. When Marines know that there is a person in the command they can talk to, this is a direct benefit to unit morale. If the chaplain believes that there is a problem in the unit the commander needs to know about, the chaplain can explain a situation such that anonymity can be preserved.

Q: What does "free exercise of religion" as per MCO 1730.6D mean?

A: It means that Marines can practice their religious beliefs without interference. MCO 1730.6D states, "Whenever possible, accommodating individual religious beliefs and practices is encouraged. However, the impact of accommodation must not adversely affect military readiness, individual or unit readiness, unit cohesion, health, safety, or good order and discipline." Common sense is the key factor. In the DOD, any religion that prescribes practices outside the limits of the UCMJ (drug use, etc.) is prohibited.

Q: If my chaplain/RP is killed or wounded in combat, how do I get a replacement?

A: You can expect the MSC chaplain to be in direct communication with the MEF and Marine Corps forces chaplains to send a replacement. Until then, the command lay leaders can assist by talking and praying with their fellow Marines.

Q: What can I expect from my chaplain/RP on the battlefield?

A: They will display the same courage and resourcefulness that you expect of your Marines.

Q: How do I accurately evaluate what my chaplain does? I am not of his faith group.

A: As an operational commander, your chaplain's faith group has almost no impact on what he does. The commander should direct both praise and concerns about their chaplain to the MSC chaplain. The MSC chaplain will likely be a captain who can help the commander mentor the chaplain. Any faith group questions can be directed to the MSC chaplain. You evaluate his effectiveness in supporting you and your Marines, not his beliefs or doctrine.

Q: Is there any special training in which my chaplain is required to regularly participate?

A: Navy chaplains are expected to attend the annual PDTC, which covers current topics in both ministry and military chaplaincy. Your chaplain is expected to attend unless he is deployed. Aboard your base, the MEF, MSC, and base chaplains will usually hold monthly or quarterly training. Your chaplain should attend these because area senior chaplains brief the junior chaplains on issues affecting ministry on the base, chaplaincy, selection boards, detailing, etc. Chaplains also are expected to attend retreats and training sponsored by their denominational endorsing agent.

Q: I have been told that chaplains are "a mixed bag." How can I know if I have a good one?

A: Is your chaplain a person of integrity? If so, then any shortfalls of knowledge or experience can be overcome. If the chaplain is lacking in character he may be able to fake it during peacetime. However when things go wrong or the unit goes to war, those with major character flaws will be exposed. In the civilian ministry there is an expression, "Until you see the church through a crisis, you are just a fill-in." The application to the military lifestyle is obvious. Ethicist Dee Hock's remarks on hiring associates apply to staff officers:

> *Hire and promote first on the basis of integrity; second, motivation; third, capacity; fourth, understanding; fifth, knowledge; and last and least, experience. Without integrity, motivation is dangerous; without motivation, capacity is impotent; without capacity, understanding is limited; without understanding, knowledge is meaningless; without knowledge, experience is blind. Experience is easy to provide and quickly put to use by people with all the other qualities.[12]*

Q: How can I develop my chaplain into a good one?

A: Allow the chaplain the same room to grow that you would give to any junior officer. If you have critical feedback, let him know. If the chaplain is teachable, he will get better.

Q: What if I have a chaplain who gets into trouble? What do I need to do? Who do I talk to?

A: First, find out what is really happening. Chaplains operate on the cutting edge of dealing with dysfunctional people. Many dysfunctional people complain about many fine chaplains (along with many fine sergeant majors and commanders). If that is the case, talk with the chaplain and get his side of the story. However, if there is a real problem and the chaplain is doing something wrong, counsel the chaplain. As with any other member of your command, if it is serious enough you should counsel him in writing. You should talk to the MSC chaplain who needs to know what is going on and can advise you about how to proceed.

Q: Should the chaplain be the FRO?

A: That is the commanding officer's call. There are several schools of thought on this. One is that if a family is resisting guidance from the FRO, as upset as they may get at the FRO, at least they will still have the chaplain to talk to. If they get mad at the chaplain then every bridge of influence and assistance has been burned. The second is that nobody works more closely with the families than the chaplain, so he is the logical choice to be the FRO.

Q: What happens on deployment stays on deployment. Why can't the chaplain understand that?

A: As Abraham Lincoln said, "You can fool some of the people all of the time, and all of the people some of the time, but you can't fool all of the people all of the time." Even without a chaplain, stories will make it home of who did what to whom. Deployment stories will come back via telephone or internet. Reality is, if you don't do anything on deployment that you wouldn't want to hear about on the 6 o'clock news, you will be okay. Even if somebody doesn't spill the beans, the impacts of deployment often come back.

Q: When we are going into battle I want the chaplain to carry a weapon. Why doesn't he want to?

A: SECNAVINST 1730.7B forbids it.

Q: My chaplain is a Roman Catholic priest. He is constantly being pulled from my unit to serve the needs of other commands. Why can't the organic chaplain take care of his/her own people?

A: Chaplains cooperate across denominational lines to provide religious ministry to all. It has to work this way for chaplains whose numbers are low density and high demand, such as Catholic priests. Whatever organization you come under, MEF or joint task force, there is a senior chaplain who is coordinating ministry on the base or in the AO. If you feel you and your chaplain are doing more than your fair share, talk to the senior chaplain.

Q: Can a chaplain conduct any kind of worship service?

A: You can expect that your Protestant chaplain can deliver a general Protestant service. Some chaplains like to do a service that is simply a "Christian" service when they are in the field. If pressed for time a chaplain with Marines should be able to perform an abbreviated service. However, a Christian chaplain cannot perform a Muslim service, or a Protestant chaplain a Catholic mass, and so on.

Q: Can a chaplain conduct weddings overseas?

A: Each overseas base has its own local regulations and laws. Marriage between two US citizens is normally not a problem. If the marriage involves an alien, the process is lengthy and difficult. However, this process can prevent impulsive weddings. MCO 1752.1C, *Marriages in Overseas Commands,* applies. The senior commander in the area will implement the regulations through local policies and procedures. These policies will include medical exams, background check, and financial counseling. Marines will be counseled in writing that a prospective alien spouse may be ineligible for admission to the United States.

Q: Why should I call the base duty chaplain for after hours emergencies when my chaplain knows my troops better?

A: The operative word is "emergency." If the commander is getting called after hours, then the unit chaplain should be called. However most of the calls that come in for the duty chaplain are not emergencies. They are complaints about everything from insurance to trash collection and they come in at all hours of the day and night. The duty chaplain can handle these calls so the unit chaplain can have some time with his family. The rule of thumb is that if the commander and entire chain of command is getting called (for a death, etc.) definitely call the unit chaplain. If not, then don't.

Q: Why should I have to fund my chaplain's temporary additional duty (TAD) for training and conferences? The MSC chaplain should be doing this.

A: The chaplain doesn't belong to the MSC chaplain. He is actually a part of your staff. If your Communications Officer goes to a school, the MSC G-6 doesn't pay for it because the Communications Officer works for you.

Q: Can chaplains earn and wear a qualification device? Shooting ribbons?

A: Yes. Chaplains may earn and wearing qualification devices such as jump wings, etc. You may see chaplains wearing Navy warfare devices such as wings, surface warfare pins, etc., they earned during prior service.

Q: Who is the real expert for knowledge about religious practices in the AO when both the chaplain and the intel officer are providing information?

A: When is comes to "soft" sciences such as anthropology, sociology, and world religions, the word "expert" should give the commander pause. The commander is encouraged to take inputs from both the chaplain and intel officer and compare them. They will have different ways of looking at an issue and real insight may be gained from listening to both of them.

Q: Will the chaplain stand duty like the rest of the officers of his grade?

A: Typically the chaplain will stand some sort of area duty. In some places it will be overnight, in some places the duty will last all week. Chaplain duty is usually a phone watch.

Q: What connections do chaplains have with their faith group and how do I support this?

A: Chaplains must maintain close ties to their faith group. Most denominations employ ministers on their staffs known as endorsing agents. Typically these individuals are retired military chaplains. Their two major functions are to screen candidates who apply to the military chaplain services and to stay in contact with military chaplains. The nature of this contact is both to answer questions and to make sure the chaplain remains a member in good standing with the endorsing body.

The commander supports his chaplain by allowing him to utilize operation and maintenance funding to attend denominational conferences, as per MCO 1730.6D.

Q: Does a Lutheran chaplain or a Baptist chaplain function as either a Lutheran or Baptist or as a sort of general duty Protestant?

A: That depends on the circumstances. When serving at a major base working in the chapel, a Lutheran may provide both a liturgical service that can be attended by Protestants that observe the liturgical calendar and a Lutheran service. A Baptist may offer both a service that non-liturgical could attend and a Baptist service. At a large base the numbers of people who would attend these services would be an indicator of their viability. Sometimes even at a large installation it doesn't make any sense to offer so many religious services that every congregation is tiny. The same dynamic has more impact at a small installation. Here the Lutheran will usually offer one liturgical service and the Baptist a non-liturgical. To split a congregation of 30 into two congregations of 15 kills the spirit of the place. Giving every group of people specialized worship services is not possible. If the chaplain is inexperienced in doing these types of services, the MSC chaplain can assist.

Q: If one of my Marines is stressed out in combat I want to send him as far away as possible. I want him to get well and I don't want his condition to affect the other Marines. Why aren't we doing this?

A: The following passage was written by a Vietnam veteran Marine and is found in MCRP 6-11C.

> *There are very few men who can be classified as cowards. Most men have too much self-respect to let their buddies down. It is the rare man indeed who will willingly violate the trust of his peers. The vast majority of men will give their lives rather than violate this trust. Proper training of combat troops, prudent leaders who are technically and tactically sound, and the reluctance of men to violate the trust of their peers are the foundation of a solid combat unit. In this environment courage and sacrifice are the rule, not the exception. At any given moment, anyone can be rendered ineffective by fear if one realizes that he is going to die. When this happens to a Marine, do not over-*

act. He knows he has let his buddies down, and he knows that his buddies and leaders know he has let them down. This is a very uncomfortable feeling for a combat Marine. The men around him will not make a big deal about his actions because they understand the situation. To make an issue of the situation will destroy the man and usually alienate the rest of your men. The man will most likely bounce back to his normal performance. The leader must keep in mind that today's coward is tomorrow's hero. If a man does not bounce back and continue to succumb to this type of fear, the Marines in his fire team will let you know when they have given up on him and no longer consider him trustworthy. Situations such as this are rare, so there is no need to make an example of the man.

Combat stress is influenced by such factors as sleep deprivation and dehydration. Research and experience has shown that sending a Marine with combat stress to the rear for 3 to 4 days and then returning him to his unit is the best option. This course of action is healing and builds self-confidence when a Marine returns to his buddies. The most damaging course of action is permanently evacuating a Marine. He will leave believing that he let his buddies down and will likely be a loss to the service. If treated near their units, 65 to 85 percent of combat stress causalities return to their units in days. About 15 to 20 percent return to duty in 1 to 2 weeks. Only about 5 to 10 percent are sent home.

The commander is encouraged to talk to the chaplain and the medical officer about the current treatment of combat stress and seek their thoughts on the mental and spiritual health of the unit.

Q: What more can we do to help our young Marines who get married?

A: Most Marine Corps bases run two programs to help married Marines. The first is the PREP. A civilian program, it is designed to run in the evenings for several weeks. Navy chaplains are trained to present PREP and have modified the material to cover to it in two, 8-hour days. PREP mainly deals with communication issues and how to solve problems without fighting; however, if the disagreement turns into a fight, how then to fight fair. Many of our young Marines come from broken homes and have never seen a functional family. Some come to PREP with the expectation that couples who "really love each other" never have disagreements. The payoff for this idea is that after the first blow-up they are "out of love" and may consider divorce. The premise that couples can fight, resolve problems, and still love each other, is new to them.

The second program comes from Marine Crops Family Team Building and is known as Lifestyle, Insights, Networking, Knowledge, and Skills (L.I.N.K.S.). Your local MCCS schedules this training.

Q: What can commanders do for newly married Marines?

A: Attend PREP with your spouse, and then talk about it at the new-join brief. The commander, chaplain, and sergeant major all need to speak realistically about what marriage in the military is like when they conduct new-join briefs. The average PFC does not see a down side to getting married. To move out of the barracks, get a pay raise, have sex, and home cooked meals seems too good to be true. Anyone trying to talk him out of this good deal must be a jerk. Too often when marriage is addressed, the young Marine feels talked down to. Addressing marriage in the military needs to have both the pros and cons brought to light. Anyone who feels he is just getting one side of the story is bound to resent what he sees as an effort to manipulate him.

Appendix A
Glossary

AO . . . . area of operations
BUMEDINST . . . . . Bureau of Medicine and Surgery instruction
CACO . . . . casualty assistance calls officer
CGRI . . . . commanding general's readiness inspection
CRB . . . . Chaplains Resource Board
CREDO . . . . Chaplains Religious Enrichment
Development Operation
CREST . . . . Chaplain and Religious Program Specialist
Expeditionary Skills Training
CRP . . . . Command Religious Program
DFC . . . . detached for cause
DNA . . . . .deoxyribonucleic acid
DOD . . . . .Department of Defense
DON . . . . Department of the Navy
EAS . . . . end of active service
FRO . . . . family readiness officer
G-6 . . . . communications and information systems officer
(major subordinate commands and
larger organizations)
IO . . . . .international organization
L.I.N.K.S. . . . Lifestyle, Insights, Networking, Knowledge, and Skills
MCO . . . . .Marine Corps order
MEF . . . . Marine expeditionary force
MOOTW . . . . military operations other than war
MSC . . . . major subordinate command
NBC . . . . nuclear, biological, and chemical
NCO . . . . noncommissioned officer
NGO . . . . nongovernmental organizations
NJP . . . . nonjudicial punishment

PDTC. . . . . .Professional Development Training Course
PFC . . . . .private first class
PME. . . . . professional military education
PREP . . . . . .Prevention and Relationship Enhancement Program
RMT . . . . .religious ministry team
RP . . . . religious program specialist
S-3 . . . . operations officer (units and organizations below
the major subordinate command level)
S-4 . . . . .logistics officer (units and organizations below
the major subordinate command level)
SECNAVINST. . . . . .Secretary of the Navy Instruction
SNCO . . . . staff noncommissioned officer
TAD. . . . . temporary additional duty
TPFDD . . . . .time-phased force and deployment data
UA . . . . unauthorized absence
UCMJ . . . . Uniform Code of Military Justice
US . . . . United States

Appendix B
References

Department of Defense Regulation

7000.14-R   Financial Management Regulations, Volume 7A, Military Pay Policies and Procedures—Active Duty and Reserve Pay

Department of Defense Instruction (DODI)

1332.40   Separation Procedures for Regular and Reserve Commission Officers

Secretary of the Navy Instruction (SECNAVINST)

1730.7B   Religious Ministry Support Within the Department of Navy

1730.8A   Accommodation of Religious Practices

1920.6B   Administrative Separation of Officers

Bureau of Medicine and Surgery Instruction (BUMEDINST)

6230.15   Immunization and Chemoprophylaxix

Navy Military Personnel Command Manual (NAVPER)

15560D   Navy Military Personnel Manual (MILPERSMAN) 1611-020, Officer Detachment for Cause (DFC)

Marine Corps Reference Publication (MCRP)

6-11C   Combat Stress

6-12A   Religious Ministry Team Handbook

Marine Corps Warfighting Publication (MCWP)

3-33.1   Marine Air-Ground Task Force Civil-Military Operations

Marine Corps Order (MCO)

1730.6D   Command Religious Programs in the Marine Corps

1752.1C   Marriages in Overseas Commands

P3040.4D   Marine Corps Casualty Procedures (Short Title: MARCORCASPROCMAN)

3574.2J   Entry Level and Sustainment Level Marksmanship Training with the M16A2 Service Rifle and M9 Service Pistol

10110.34E   US Marine Corps Food Service and Subsistence Program

Appendix C
Notes

1. T. R. Fehrenbach, *This Kind Of War* (New York, NY: Bantam Books, 1991) p. 349.

2. E. B. Sledge, *With The Old Breed At Peleliu and Okinawa* (Navato, CA: Presidio Press, 1981) p. 267.

3. Sledge, p. 123, 124.

4. Karen Montor, ed. *Naval Leadership: Voices of Experience* (Annapolis, MD: Naval Institute Press, 1978) p. 462.

5. James Toner, *True Faith and Allegiance: The Burden of Military Ethics* (Lexington: University of Kentucky, 1995) p. 61.

6. Daniel Goleman, *Emotional Intelligence* (New York: Bantam Books, 1995).

7. Harry Spiller, *Scars of Vietnam* (Jefferson NC: McFarland & Company, Inc., 1994) p. 10, 11.

8. Captain Clifford M. Drury, CHC, USNR, Bureau of Naval Personnel, Washington DC, *The History of the Chaplain Corps, Volume One 1778-1939,* 1883, p. 235.

9. Commander Herrbert Bergsma, CHC, USN, *Chaplains with Marines in Vietnam 1962-1971*, History And Museums Divisions, HQMC, Washington DC, 1985, 163.

10. Carl von Clausewitz, *On War* (Princeton: University Press, 1976) p. 189.

11. Sledge, 283-84.

12. Dee Hock, *Fast Company*, Issue 5, Oct 1996, p. 79.

www.ingramcontent.com/pod-product-compliance
Lightning Source LLC
Chambersburg PA
CBHW021913040426

42447CB00007B/837